HAVE YOU EVER SEEN A
BLUE WHALE?
ANIMAL BOOK AGE 4

Children's Animal Books

BABY PROFESSOR
EDUCATION KIDS

Speedy Publishing LLC
40 E. Main St. #1156
Newark, DE 19711
www.speedypublishing.com

The largest animals that have ever existed are swimming around in the ocean right now! Read on and learn about blue whales.

Blue Whale (balaenoptera musculus).

A BIG BLUE WHALE

We think about dinosaurs being big, and some of them were. But the biggest dinosaur we know about weighed less than 100 tons. An average grownup blue whale weighs almost twice that much!

Blue Whale (Balaenoptera musculus).

Blue whales are marine mammals, like seals and walruses. That means they started out as land animals millions of years ago, and evolved over time for living in the ocean. If you ever see the skeleton of a whale, you can find the little tiny bones that are all that remain of the legs whales had when they lived on the land!

Blue whale diving in the Sea of Cortez, Baja California, Mexico.

Blue whales are up to 100 feet long. Their skin is sort of blue-gray on the top of their bodies, and this gives them their name. The underside of the whale is sort of a grayish-yellow, and sailors in the nineteenth century called them *"Sulphur Bottoms"* because of that color.

Blue whale dives down in a fluking motion.

For their size, whales are slim and efficient. They are made to be able to move smoothly through the water. They can travel at about ten miles per hour, but can race along at about twice that speed when they need to, for a short distance. When they are feeding, they go much more slowly.

Drawing of marine mammals. Blue whale, Sperm whale, Dolphin and Orca (killer whale).

The whale's head is flat, with a long ridge running from the top of its upper lip up to the two blowholes on the top of its head. The blowhole is where the whale blows out stale air and takes in fresh air when it comes to the surface to breathe. Since it's not a fish, the whale can't get air directly from the water.

When the whale blows out the stale air, it makes a fountain of air and mist that goes as much as thirty feet up.

The whale's flippers are about ten feet long. They help the whale swim and change direction.

Blue Whale

WHERE THEY LIVE AND WHAT THEY DO

Blue whales used to live everywhere in almost every ocean on Earth. There are a lot fewer of them now than there used to be, because people hunted them for their oil. Before gasoline and kerosene were available, whale oil was a very popular fuel for lamps and even for heating.

Blue Whale near Mirrisa, Sri Lanka.

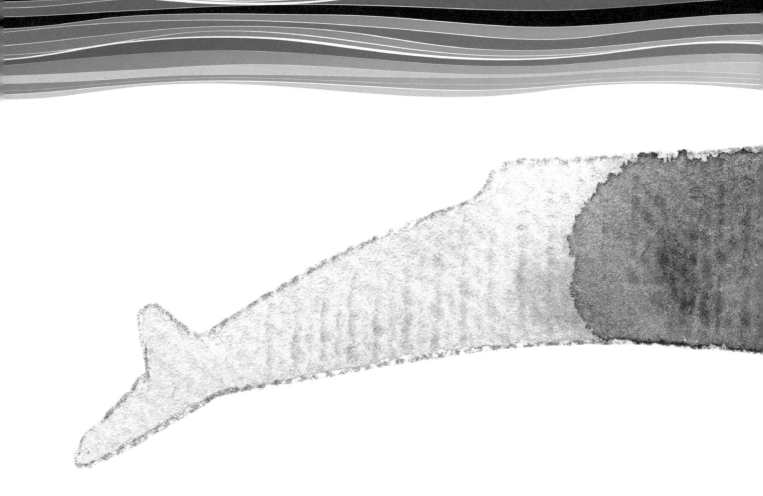

Most adult blue whales live on their own, or with one other whale. Nobody knows how long those pairs of whales stay together. If there is a lot of good food in

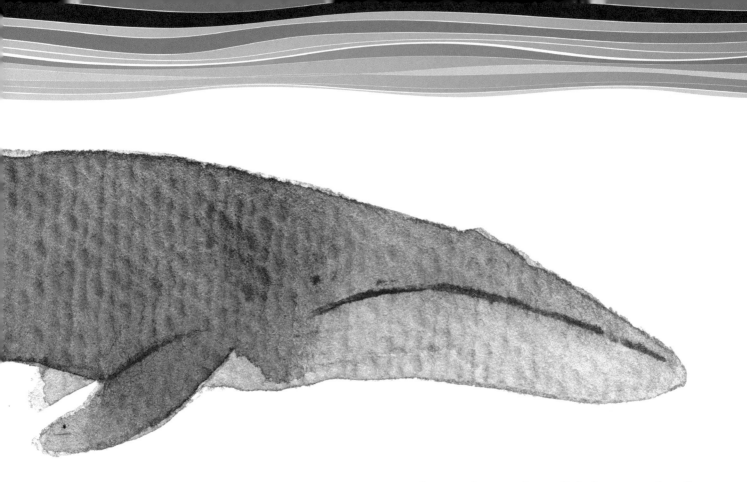

Watercolor sketch of blue whale.

part of the ocean, there may be up to fifty blue whales in one area; but they go their separate ways once the good food is used up.

Large Blue Whale off Southern California coast.

While they travel, blue whales usually swim about 40 feet below the surface. This takes them below the effect of waves on the surface, and lets them swim faster with less effort. It also means it is harder for scientists to track blue whales, so we still don't know a lot about where they go at different times in the year!

EATING

The whale's mouth is large, to suit its body. Inside its mouth are hundreds of screens made of material called baleen, instead of teeth. The whale takes in huge amounts of water, and all the sea creatures that are sucked in with the water get caught on the baleen screens. The whale then gets rid of the water and licks the food off the screens with its tongue.

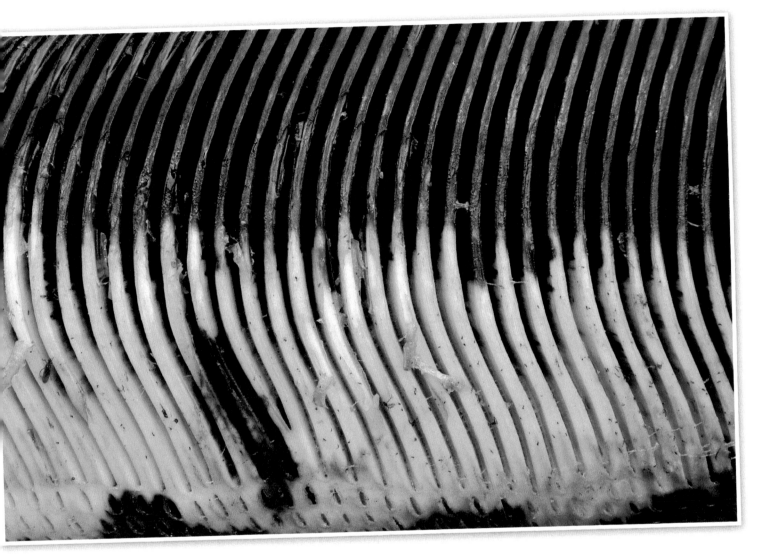

Whale Baleen

It's the biggest creature that ever lived on Earth, but most of the blue whale's food is tiny: it mainly eats krill, little creatures that are related to (and look a little like) lobsters. Of course, it takes a lot of krill to keep a blue whale going: an adult whale probably eats almost two tons of krill every day.

Whale Baleen

Blue whales travel to the Antarctic at certain times of the year, when there are a lot of krill, and eat and eat and eat, storing up lots of energy. A whale that arrives in the feeding grounds weighing about 100 tons can leave weighing about 150 tons! Then they use this energy over the rest of the year as they travel through waters where there is less food.

Whale Feeding.

Zoo plankton in the ocean.

When feeding, the whale dives to about 300 feet, and can stay down for ten or twenty minutes before coming up for fresh air. It swims through the groups of krill, sucking them in with the sea water and filtering out the food.

Krill in the Ocean.

Blue whales are happy to eat squid and small fish they catch by accident, but they can't eat big fish or other creatures. They have no teeth to chew their food with, and their throats are small for their bodies: they can't swallow anything much larger than a beach ball.

MOTHERS AND BABIES

A blue whale mother has a baby (a "calf") once every two or three years, after carrying the baby for about a year. The calf weighs almost three tons and is over twenty feet long when it is born! That makes a new-born blue whale bigger than almost any other adult animal

Cartoon Illustration of Mother Whale and Baby.

The mother blue whale feeds her baby milk, the way mammals on land do. The baby whale drinks up to 150 gallons of milk a day! After about six months, when the baby whale is twice the size it was at birth, it is able to feed itself on krill.

Blue Whale 3D image.

STAYING ALIVE

Since whales are so large, only human hunters are a serious threat to them. Killer whales are the other threat, mainly attacking young whales. About one blue whale in four has scars it got when being attacked by a killer whale.

Killer Whale

We don't know how long a blue whale can live, if hunters don't interfere with it. Scientists can estimate the age of a whale by looking at the build-up of wax in a whale's ear (sort of like looking at the rings of a tree to see how old it is). It is obviously a little hard to do this on a living

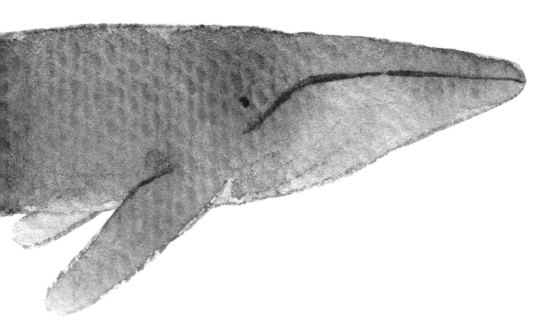

whale, so the scientists work on the bodies of whales who have died. The layers of wax can build up to more than ten inches deep. The oldest whale measured this way was over one hundred years old, but blue whales' average life span is probably about eighty years.

ARE THEY IN DANGER?

Blue whales were hunted so heavily during the nineteenth and twentieth centuries that they almost became extinct. Before the whalers started hunting them, there were large groups of as many as 300,000 blue whales in different parts of the world. Now the world blue whale population is below 25,000, and the largest group is less than two thousand whales.

Blue Whale being hunted by old time whalers.

Most countries have stopped hunting whales and so the numbers have stopped falling. But the blue whale population has a long way to go before it gets back to its pre-hunting numbers.

A Blue Whale skeleton lying on the beach at the location of an abandoned whale processing facility.

A Blue whale (Balaenoptera musculus), seen near the Farallon Island near San Francisco, is the largest species on Earth.

THEY ARE BIG!

Nobody has ever weighed a complete blue whale, because they are just too big. But here are some fun facts about their size:

- Blue whales who live in the northern waters of the Atlantic and Pacific oceans tend to be smaller than the whales who live around the Antarctic. But even the northern whales are far larger than any dinosaur ever was.

Blue Whale Back.

Blue Whale Illustration.

- The longest blue whale ever measured was over 100 feet from mouth to tail.

- Females are usually a little longer than males, but male blue whales are a little heavier than females of the same length. The males have more muscle mass and denser bones.

The Museum of Natural History in Gothenburg, Sweden contains the only stuffed blue whale in the world.

- A blue whale's tongue weighs more than three tons, more than what an average elephant weighs.

- The whale's mouth can hold almost 100 tons of food and water at one time.

- A blue whale's heart weighs about 400 pounds and is the largest heart of any animal species. You can hear the heart beating from as much as two miles away, and it only beats about ten times a minute.

Blue whale diving in the Indian Ocean, south of Sri Lanka.

The Blue Whale is the largest animal known to have existed.

- Blue whales have a relatively small brain for their size, but it is highly convoluted, or wrinkled. The wrinkles increase the brain's surface area, the number of neurons it has, and the amount of work the brain can do.

- Blue whale calves grow quickly! They gain as much as 200 pounds every day while they are nursing. And even when they are born, they are as large as an adult hippopotamus!

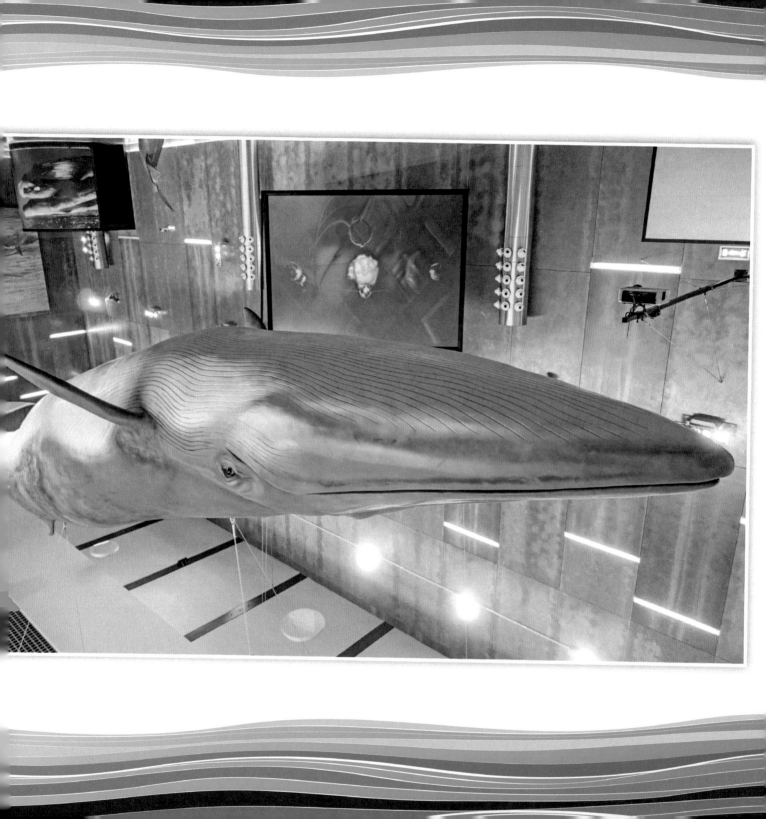

- Blue whales are noisy. But they make their moans, groans, and other noises at a frequency that is so low that human ears can't hear the noise. Other whales can hear the sounds though, from as much as one thousand miles away!

Museu da Baleia (Whale Museum). Huge Blue Whale model hanging from ceiling.

- One of the other causes of blue whale deaths are collisions with large ships. An unknown number of whales are killed or injured this way every year. In stories like *Moby-Dick,* whales attack ships. In real life, it is usually the ship that hurts the whale.

FASCINATING ANIMALS

In the air and the water, and on the land, we share this Earth with lots of amazing animals. Read about more of them in Baby Professor books like *The Great White Shark, Endangered Mammals from Around the World,* and *Who Lives in the Barren Desert?*

Blue Whale at Ocean Hall of the American Museum of Natural History (AMNH)

Visit

BABY PROFESSOR
EDUCATION KIDS

www.BabyProfessorBooks.com

to download Free Baby Professor eBooks
and view our catalog of new and exciting
Children's Books

Made in the USA
Monee, IL
23 September 2021